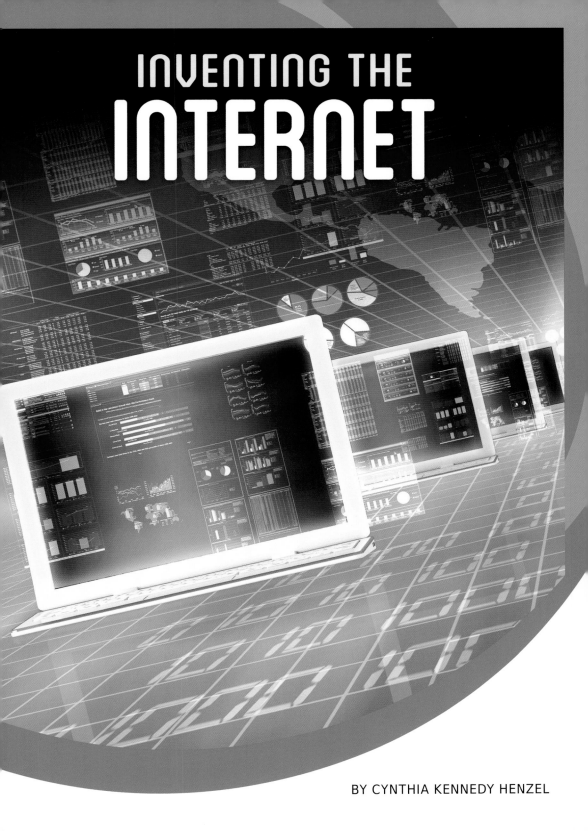

INVENTING THE
INTERNET

BY CYNTHIA KENNEDY HENZEL

Published by The Child's World®
1980 Lookout Drive • Mankato, MN 56003-1705
800-599-READ • www.childsworld.com

Acknowledgments
The Child's World®: Mary Berendes, Publishing Director
Red Line Editorial: Design, editorial direction, and production
Photographs ©: Shutterstock Images, cover, 1, 18; Philip Preston/Boston Globe/Getty
Images, 4; NASA, 6; Reed Saxon/AP Images, 8; Aleshkovsky Mitya/ITAR-TASS Photo/
Corbis, 11; Roger Ressmeyer/Corbis, 12; Elise Amendola/AP Images/Corbis, 15; Kim
Kulish/Corbis, 16; Lisa Strachan/iStockphoto, 20

ISBN 9781634074575

LCCN 2015946291

Printed in the United States of America
PA02370

ABOUT THE AUTHOR

Cynthia Kennedy Henzel has a BS in social studies education and an MS in
geography. She has worked as a teacher-educator and is currently a partner
at an Internet strategy consulting firm. She has written more than 50 books
for young people.

TABLE OF
CONTENTS

Chapter 1

CAUGHT OFF GUARD

Scientist J. C. R. Licklider frowned at the stacks of papers on his desk. It was the 1950s. Licklider was studying how the brain understands sound. But he had a problem. He spent most of his time looking for information. Instead, he wanted to spend his time thinking about his studies. He had a solution. He dreamed of a network of computers. On this network, he would send and receive information. Information would be easy to find and see. He called his idea the Intergalactic Network.

Licklider's dream got a jump start in 1957. That year, the Soviet Union launched *Sputnik*. It was the first man-made satellite. People in the United States panicked. They were falling behind in technology.

In response, the U.S. government created the Advanced Research Projects Agency (ARPA). This agency would speed up research in technology. ARPA was part of the Department of Defense. The department's leaders worried about enemies

◀ J. C. R. Licklider in his office

▲ Two people work at an early computer.

destroying U.S. communications. So, they wanted a reliable way to send information across the country.

In 1962, Licklider went to work for ARPA to solve this problem. He remembered his dream of an Intergalactic Network. Maybe the government needed a computer network!

At this time, computers were very large. One computer filled an entire room. They were used to solve difficult math problems. People sometimes sent data from one computer to another. But this process was difficult and slow. A modem sent data over a telephone line. It took a long time to send large amounts of data in one telephone call. Plus, telephone lines were not reliable. Sometimes computers did not receive all the data.

Two researchers solved this problem at the same time. They were Paul Baran in the United States and Donald Davies in the United Kingdom. The solution was called packet-switching.

Packet-switching breaks data into small packets. Each packet is the same size. A computer sends the data by routing the packets through a network of computers. The computer that receives the packets puts them back together. Routing packets is like moving a building by taking it apart. The pieces are labeled and packed onto different trucks. The trucks take different routes. They arrive at different times. When all the pieces get to the new location, they are put back together.

Moving data over many different routes is much faster than moving over one telephone line. A network of many computers means more routes for data to travel. This makes communication more reliable. The invention gave ARPA what it needed to create the first computer network. Would it work? Licklider thought so. In the 1960s, he wrote, "In a few years, men will be able to communicate more effectively through a machine than face to face."[1]

Chapter 2

FROM ARPANET TO INTERNET

Robert Taylor became head of computer research at ARPA in 1965. He kept working on a computer network. He hired Larry Roberts to design it. They called the network ARPAnet.

But Taylor had a problem. Many universities and companies did not want to join a network. They had big, expensive computers. They didn't want to share them. And they didn't want to make changes to their computers.

Taylor was firm. Everyone had to work together to make ARPAnet a success. Taylor said places that didn't join ARPAnet would not get money for new computers. At last, they agreed to join.

Each node, or point on the network, got a small computer. These small computers did the routing. They were easily hooked up to the big computers that stored data.

◀ **Leonard Kleinrock shows the computer he used to send the first message over ARPAnet.**

By 1969, the ARPA team was ready to send a message. The team set up four nodes. Three were in California. One was in Utah. Leonard Kleinrock had worked on creating the network. He was now at the University of California, Los Angeles (UCLA). The team decided to send the first message from UCLA in Southern California to Stanford Research Institute in Northern California.

Teams at both locations gathered near their computers. Everyone was ready. At UCLA, team member Charles Kline attempted to log in to the Stanford computer. He typed an L. Over the phone, the team in Stanford said they saw the L. Kline typed an O. Again, the Stanford team saw the letter. Kline typed a G. Without warning, the Stanford computer crashed! But the team did not give up. They soon fixed the problem. They sent the first message: LOGIN.

In the 1970s, ARPAnet added more nodes. The network grew. Information zipped from computer to computer all over the country. Licklider's dream was coming true! Soon, other groups created separate networks. But now ARPA had a new problem. A person on one network could not communicate with a person on a different network.

The ARPA team went back to work. They needed a protocol, or set of rules, to send information between different networks. ARPA team members Robert Kahn and Vint Cerf

▲ Vint Cerf later became a vice president at Google.

created protocols for all networks to use. These protocols are still used today. The Internet protocol (IP) gives an address to each computer. The transmission control protocol (TCP) tells computers how to send packets.

The new network of networks got a new name. It was called the Internet. It connected universities, governments, and large companies. But computers were still expensive and difficult to use. They were not available to most people. But that would soon change.

Chapter 3

CAUGHT IN THE WEB

Steve Wozniak liked to tinker with things. By the 1970s, he was trying to build a computer. He soon joined with Steve Jobs. Jobs liked to work on computers, too. But he was also a great businessman. In 1977, Wozniak and Jobs introduced the Apple II computer. The Apple II was inexpensive. It was easy to set up and use. This was important because most people had never seen a computer. Apple II was a great success. Soon, people were e-mailing, writing, and playing games on computers.

Then a businessman named Steve Case had a big idea. He wanted people to use the Internet for social media. But people needed a way to help them connect with others online. Case introduced America Online (AOL) in the late 1980s. Millions of people signed up for his service. People could join groups and chat with others online. But AOL made people pay to join in the conversation.

◄ Steve Wozniak sits with an Apple II computer.

Tim Berners-Lee didn't like this. He was a computer scientist from England who worked at a lab in Switzerland. Berners-Lee wanted to make the Internet more like a library. He imagined a "space where you can communicate through sharing information."[2] So, he went to work.

Berners-Lee wrote protocols for sharing information. It's the way the Internet is used today. Every **Web page** uses a language called HTML. Every Web page has an address called a URL. Web pages use a protocol called HTTP. HTTP lets users click on a special word or picture called a link. The link takes users to another Web page.

Berners-Lee called the new system the World Wide Web. In 1991, he put up the first Web page. Today, many people think the Internet and the Web are the same thing. But they are not. The Internet connects computers. The Web connects people.

Berners-Lee did not make money from his invention. He gave the Web to the world. No person, company, or government controls it. Anyone can put information on the Web or pull information from it. Anyone can create new ways to use it. This freedom changed the world.

Chapter 4

THE INTERNET GOES WILD

In the 1990s, the Web was a new frontier. To many people, it was a virtual Wild West. People flocked online to create thousands of businesses. Some of these people, like Marc Andreessen, invented tools to make the Web easier to use. In the mid-1990s, he created the Netscape browser. A browser pulls information from the Web so that people can view it. Tim Berners-Lee had made a Web browser in the early 1990s. But Netscape was easier to use.

Other people put up Web sites to sell music, books, and other things. They put up Web sites to communicate. They put up **blogs** for news and entertainment. By 1997, more than one million Web sites had been created. With so many Web sites, people had trouble finding what they wanted. At first, people tried making lists of Web sites. But more Web sites appeared every day.

◀ Larry Page (top) and Sergey Brin (bottom) at Google's headquarters in Mountain View, California

▲ By 2015, Wikipedia had more than 4.8 million articles in English.

Larry Page and Sergey Brin found an answer. They were math students at Stanford University in California. They wrote a complicated formula. The formula determined the importance of a Web site. Now, people could search for a topic. In the results, the most important Web sites were at the top of the list. Page and Brin called their new searching software Google. Now, people could quickly find the information they needed.

Lots of people were making money on the Web. But others were still interested in Berners-Lee's dream of a free online library. In 2001, Jimmy Wales and Larry Sanger started the Web site Wikipedia. On the site, anyone can write about a subject. Other people can add new information.

Many people did not think this free encyclopedia would work. Who would write for free? How could readers know that the information was true? But millions of people added information to Wikipedia. Most people tried to be accurate. Today, Wikipedia is one of the world's most-used Web sites.

People today depend on the Web. Users find information and entertainment. The Web is a place for shopping and sharing videos. People find new friends and keep in touch with old ones. The Internet connects billions of people around the world. But some people believe this is just the beginning.

THE WEB TAKES OFF

Year	Number of Web Sites
1991 (Aug. 6)	1
1995	23,500
1999	3,177,453
2003	40,912,332
2007	121,892,559
2011	346,004,403
2015 (Aug.)	987,323,542

Chapter 5

INTO THE FUTURE

People started to wonder what else the Internet could be used for. They knew computers were now small enough to be on tiny **chips**. These chips allowed smartphones to access the Internet. But what if the chips could be put into other things?

These inventors came up with an idea called the Internet of Things. Someday, everyday objects could be linked to the Internet. A refrigerator could send a message to a person's phone when he needed more milk. An umbrella could be linked to a weather Web site. The umbrella would know when it was going to rain. It could say, "Take me!" as a person left the house.

Some people don't want to rely on other people's inventions. They like to make things themselves. These people are called makers. Makers create new games. They program robots. They create and share art and music.

J. C. R. Licklider's dream came true. Now, makers are forming dreams of their own.

◀ In the future, chips are likely to be even smaller.

GLOSSARY

blogs (BLAWGZ): Blogs are online journals where people share personal stories or ideas. Blogs can be about many topics, including cooking, movies, and video games.

chips (CHIPS): Chips are small electronic circuits that can send information. Smartphones have chips inside them.

modem (MOH-dum): A modem is a machine that changes the signal from one kind of machine so that it can be understood by another kind of machine. A computer modem is used to connect a computer to a telephone.

network (NET-wurk): A network is a system of computers connected together. The Internet is a network.

routing (ROUT-ing): Routing means sending something along a particular path. The computer is routing the message through India.

social media (SO-shul MEE-dee-uh): Social media are Web sites that provide places for people to share personal ideas and information. He got ideas for the party from social media.

Web page (WEB payj): A Web page is a document connected to the World Wide Web. She found a Web page about using the Internet.

TO LEARN MORE

Books

Brasch, Nicolas. *The Internet*. Mankato, MN: Smart Apple Media, 2011.

Smibert, Angie. *12 Great Moments that Changed Internet History*. Mankato, MN: Peterson, 2015.

Yomtov, Nel. *Internet Inventors*. New York: Children's Press, 2013.

Web Sites

Visit our Web site for links about the Internet:
childsworld.com/links

Note to Parents, Teachers, and Librarians: We routinely verify our Web links to make sure they are safe and active sites. So encourage your readers to check them out!

SOURCE NOTES

1. J. C. R. Licklider and Robert Taylor. "The Computer as a Communication Device." *Kurzweil Accelerating Intelligence.* KurzweilAINetwork, 9 Nov. 2001. Web. 13 Aug. 2015.

2. "Web's Inventor Gets a Knighthood." *BBC.* BBC, 31 Dec. 2003. Web. 13 Aug. 2015.

INDEX